READING OLD HANDWR

How to start

Probably the first time you will come face to face with older styles of handwriting is in parish registers – in fact, they are a good way of cutting your teeth, since what the entries say is partly predictable. It is much more difficult to start cold on whole slabs of prose where you are not sure even of what kind of document it is, and certainly not what phrases to expect.

When you are given a set of registers or a microfilm, the natural reaction is to begin at the beginning. This is one of those rules which should be overturned in family history – always begin at the end. There are three good reasons for this: in the first place, what you know already is likely to involve the end of the registers, since we work back from what we know to what we don't know. In the second place, as you work back, you acquire more knowledge, in particular of which other families your ancestors married into – making them henceforth 'yours' to be collected; in the third place, the writing of those early registers is strange and unless you ease yourself into it by getting familiar with the surnames occurring in the parish, you could fail to identify the relevant names among so many new ones and have to work back over them again. A seventeenth century register can look totally unreadable, at first sight, but if you have trained on the later years you will find names emerging from the general scribble which are the ones you want.

Even Victorian registers can present some problems, owing mainly to bad writing or personal styles. And as you go back, the choice may be between the round hand of the parish clerk, with spellings which startle you, or the crabbed hand of the clergyman. As with modern handwriting, some people have evolved styles which are very much their own, with some letters not quite like anyone else's.

However, we are able to read their communications now because the whole word can only be one thing, despite the strange squiggle in the middle. And this is an advantage we have in reading older hand-writings – the single letters may look difficult, but in combination, they make sense.

I have included here a number of different forms for individual letters in handwritings common in three centuries – and you will at once see that the shapes of different letters may be very similar, but the person who writes the form of *c* which looks like an *r* has a distinct version of *r* which he uses. It is just a matter of picking out what that individual has selected as his own form of an alphabet.

Capital letters tend to give the most trouble, since there is more scope for individual choice here. The trick here is to study the capitals in Christian names and then pick out the same letter in surnames. Sometimes the body of the word is quite clear, and only the peculiar bundle of strokes at the beginning throws you for the moment.

I have included alphabets for different periods, but these can only be approximately dated, since a lot depends on the age of the man writing. An elderly clergyman, educated in the 1680s, does not suddenly change his style since he happens to be recording events of the 1730s. Even young clerks tended to experiment with the writing of a former age when they were recording important events. In modern times, scrolls of honour have often been written in 'Gothic' lettering and wedding invitations printed in 'Old English' style. The recipients can generally work out the odder looking letters, because they know what it ought to be saying. The same applies to older documents – once you know the phrasing to expect, you can read the words. It is just a matter of breaking yourself in on the more readable documents and then tackling the ones that look as of they are in Greek at first sight.

'Victorian Vicars' and 'Shy Young Curates'

The bulk of nineteenth century registers are in familiar writing, and if the books were kept by parish clerks, you will generally have no problems. They were taught a round hand style of penmanship, similar to modern writing, with a few odder capitals. The most obvious thing you will meet is the use, by persons educated in the first half of the century, of the 'long *s*'. This is used extensively in words with **ss**, like **Miss** and **dressmaker** and **permission**, and cheap comedians still raise a weak laugh by pronouncing it as *f*. It was an American genealogist who not only read **ss** as **p** but proceeded to inform a client that her good Yorkshire ancestor was a **drepmaker**, meaning that she made drapes, which is American for curtains.

Documents penned by more highly educated people tend to give more trouble. The more used a person was to writing, the less neat it was (think of prescriptions).

There is a skinny, pinched up style which reminds me of pale young curates, scared of expressing themselves floridly.   In this style, the round letters are flattened, especially in *e*, *o*, *l*, *h*; *b*, *g* and the capital letters are similarly emaciated.   It is as if they were issued with a tiny pen and a small bottle of cheap ink and ordered to make it last for a year.

Some of the cross strokes were not heavy enough to come out - and there is very little distinction between *u* and *n* when the horizontal bar is almost lost; or between *in* and *m*, or *rr* if the dot vanishes. An incomplete top curve sometimes causes trouble, resulting in an *a* which looks like *u* and a *d* which could be *cl*.

Gandy

Crauford

Staines/
Hames/Harris

Jane

dear/clear

The problem capitals are *S* and *L*, which look remarkably similar, causing readers to claim a *Lawyer* as ancestor when he was a *Sawyer*, or to read *Saunders* as *Launders*:

Saunders

and the curate's limp *R* with hardly any waist, which looks like an *N*:

Rogation   *Reeve*

The minimally written *H* with the central bar reduced to a feeble tick on the second upright could be *It* or *If*. Commonsense generally sorts it out, but I have seen *Hutt* misread as *Iliett*.

Hutt   *Head*   *Stead*

St at the beginning of a word, if reduced, can look very like an *H*; and *vice versa*.

Stanley

There are numerous pairs of names where this causes trouble:-
Stanley and *Hanley*, *Stewart* and *Hewart*, and, with a pinched *o*, *Stocks* and *Hicks*. Commonsense will not help you sort these out, but a knowledge of the common names in the parish may.

J and *I*, *T* and *F* all look very similar, in all styles of writing, and the less curved they are the more the chance of confusion. This has resulted in a name originally written as *Instone* being copied into the St. Catherine's indexes of marriages as *Justone*.

Instone

The more expansive style (the florid vicar) is always in a hurry, and runs letters together or trails ink across one letter on his way to the next, rather than take the pen off or go down to the base of the line before starting the next one.   The result is confusion between *i*, *m*, *n*, *u*; between *le* and *b*, *gu* and *gri*, *K* and *R*; and the *J*, *I*, *T*, *F* group above.

The florid *H* has been read as *Th*, *St*, *If*.   The florid openwork *B* looks very like an *M.*

If St If M   Barton

                                                        Barton

The solution is to get familiar with the surnames in the parish, and then see what the writers make of them in their better moments, which gives a clue to the worst scrawls. If in doubt, see if the name occurs again lower down. If it doesn't, make a careful copy of it - sometimes the very act of doing this makes it all plain. Don't trace from an actual document without permission from the archivist, who will usually provide acetate to work over, so the pencil doesn't make a dent in the page.

Compare the marriage registers, where a surname can occur in isolation, with the baptismal registers shortly afterwards. There you should be able to locate the name and set it against a similarly written letter where there is no doubt of the interpretation. Bless all the Victorian *Henry* s and *Harry* s for deciding what is an *H* and what is *St*; the *John Thomas* s and the many *Isaac* s and *Frederick* s who show the forms of those initials.

Numbers up

Figures which often cause problems to the G.R.O. staff (resulting in wrongly interpreted certificates) and in reading censuses are *6* and *8*, which look very similar in the 'open' state, and *5*, which has only to lose its top knot to read as *6*. The curate's *7* can read as *1*, and so can a really mingy *3.*

1 7   2 2 2 3 3 1 4 4 4 5 6 5 6 6 7 1 8 6 6 9 4 9

When Married.	Name and Surname.	Age.	Condition.	Rank or Profession
December 24ᵗʰ	James Gates	21.	Bachelor	Labourer
	Anne Smith	21.	Spinster	Labourer

d in the _Parish Church_ _____according to the Rites and Ceremonies of the _Esta..._

arriage { *James Gates* _____ } — in the
is   { *Anne Smith her X mark* _____ } Presence
nized   {   } of us,
en us,   {

An example of nineteenth century handwriting.

An alphabet of around **1800.**

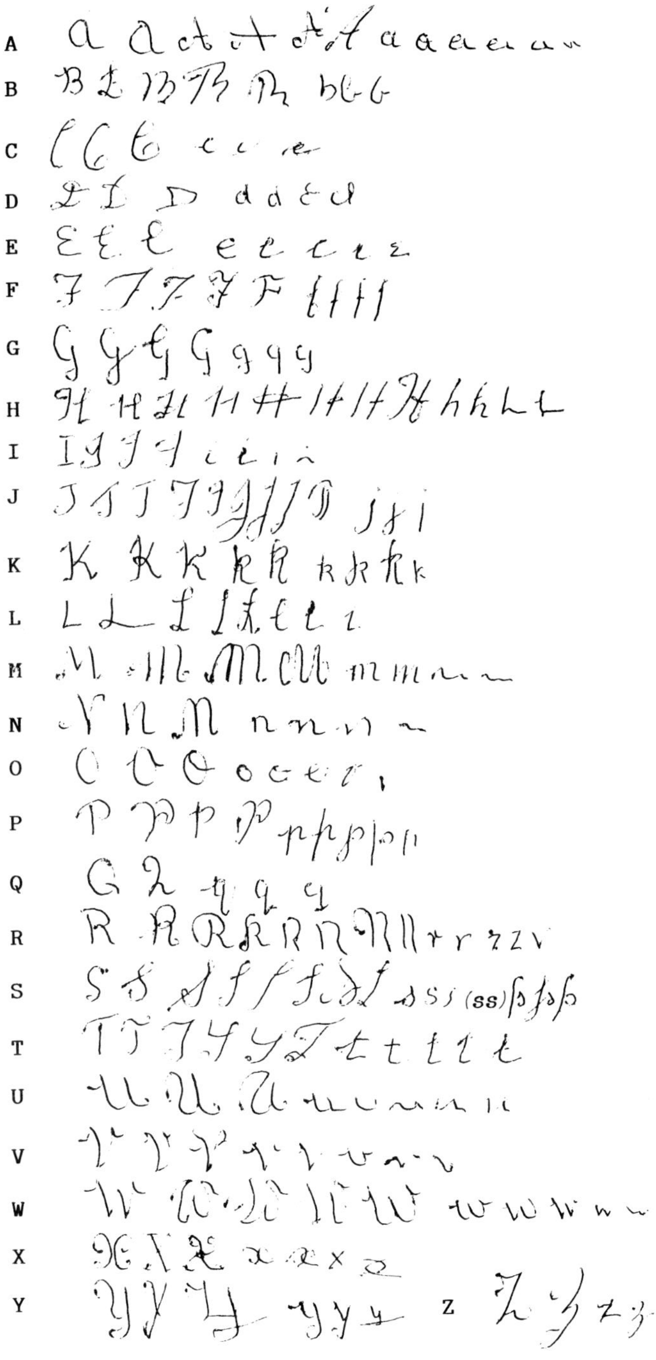

The Eighteenth Century

The second stage of the register usually searched will be the Hardwicke Act marriage registers, from 1754 to 1812, and the baptismal and burial registers from about 1700, which accompany them. Again, working backwards in sections of fifty years or so is recommended, so that you become familiar with the surnames involved. Before 1733, you may meet Latinised entries, to add to the problems of reading. Although the use of Latin in official documents was then stopped, you do occasionally meet a perverse clergyman who carried on using it (see *Simple Latin for Family Historians*, in this series, back cover).

The nearer you get to 1700, the more likely you are to find really odd writing, for clergy educated well before the end of the century did not adapt to the modern style.   Neither did the teachers.   This example of two receipts for payment of their salaries by a middle aged female and a young male teacher in 1717 shows how she clung to, and presumably taught, an older style of writing, with 'plum' *C*s and a closed *e*.

You will normally meet with the long *s* in the middle of a word, and sometimes at the beginning – never at the end, unless as the first of a double *ss*.

Small *e* is frequently like an *o* with a large loop at the top. As time goes by, it breaks open into the modern type of *e*, but some writers opened it on the wrong side, especially at the end of words. Clergy may use the Greek *e*.

An *o* should be a simple circle, but sometimes you will find a tiny loop in the top, smaller than the *e* loop.

There is an awkward habit of leaving the *t* uncrossed, or making the join to the next letter do as a cross bar. To compensate for this, a final double *ll* very often *is* crossed. Here your experience of local names will tell you if *Gravell* or *Gravett* is intended.

The upright of small *d* curls back over the previous letter, sometimes into it. Small *p* is often split, with two uprights. Small *c* may lack a top bar (or have one tacked on as an afterthought) so that it looks like an *r*, but if so, *r* is either doubled, or has a definite top curl.

An
alphabet
of
around
1700.

A

B

C

D

E

F

G

H

I/J

K

L   (final)

M

N

O

P

Q

R

S   (Initial medial)   (final)

T

U/V

W

X

Y

Z

The short uprights of *n*, *u*, *m* and *i* look very much the same, and if the dot goes missing, you will have to try alternatives.

Small *u* and *v* are totally interchangeable usually with *v* at the beginning and *u* in the middle of words.

given

unto

u, v

Capital letters cause most difficulties, since they may be written in an older style that the rest of the text, for show. Refer to the next section if in doubt. Wild extra curves are added, especially on gentry names. If the letter is in a surname, check it against Christian names on the same page.

Capital *F* is frequently written as two little *ff*s joined, which causes ignorant people to adopt this as the 'correct' spelling of their name. Always transcribe as *F*. It should have a central bar and sometimes a 'top hat'.

There is usually no distinction between *J* and *I*, and very little between those and *T* and *F* in different hands. Each writer has his own way of distinguishing – if he wants to. A *J* may have a small cross bar or tick projecting left, and an *F* a definite bar jutting right, sometimes so definite it has been read as *Tr*.

Skinny *S*'s cause the same problems as in the nineteenth century, with confusion between *Sl* or *St* and *H*, taken in isolation. Fortunately, they usually look different in the same man's writing. Weak strokes of the pen may have allowed the ink to flake away, losing curves and crosses once there.   Ultra violet light, available at many record offices, may show up what was written there.

It is easy to see how mistakes in parish registers may have arisen. If the clerk wrote down in his 'rough book' the christening of John son of John and Margaret Smith as
bp Jno son of Jno and Marg. Smith
it was very easy for the parson to read it later as
bp Tho son of Tho and Mary Smith
and expand the name to **Thomas**.

John for **Thomas**, **Mary** for **Margaret**, **Sarah** for **Hanah**, and *vice versa* are commonplace.

The real problem comes with the writing of those who rarely do it – perhaps just signing the marriage register.   The names of groom and bride will be repeated in the handwriting of the clerk or clergyman, but deciphering the laborious scrawl of the witnesses is harder. The temptation is to ignore these, but often they are relatives, whose names may settle a question of identity. Checking with the baptismal registers to find out the clerk's version may help to discover what the scratches, apparently made by an angry cat, mean.

In some cases, when the clergyman takes over the register entries from the clerk, the standard of spelling may (or may not) improve, but the writing gets more convoluted. It may help to compare the register with the Bishop's transcript, to see if one is written more legibly than the other.

The standard of writing in wills may decline in the provinces, but their value as genealogical documents is great, and it pays to get a photocopy and study it at leisure, using your knowledge of the standard phrases, with which most older wills begin, to help untangle the useful information. If there are both an original will and a register copy, comparison of the two may make things clear. However, sometimes the clerk making the copy was unfamiliar with the names of the people and places and got it wrong. Poor quality ink, which has faded, does not help, but a good photostat may improve the contrast here.

Once you know what to expect in an old will, you will realise that most of the first six or more lines can be scanned and you do not need to concentrate hard unless they seem to be significantly different from the norm. It is only when you get to *Imprimis* (at first) or *Item*, where the listing of legacies begins, that you need to read with close attention.

All swags and flounces

In reading documents created by people who learned to write from 1600 onwards, practice makes perfect. There was a very considerable variety of writing style, and it is not the age of the document so much as the personal habit of the writer which makes it hard or easy to read what he has written. There is too the condition of the document and ink to contend with. Sometimes the ink has flaked away, and it is helpful to put the page under ultra-violet light. A photostat may bring up a darker image than the original.

Although the potential writer of documents was taught a neat 'secretary hand' for that purpose and there was a modern looking pointed 'Italian' hand in common use, the great temptation was to ornament these with unnecessary swags and flounces to make the writing look more important. It was a case of education being seen to be had. The headings and first words of paragraphs are often fancier than the rest, sometimes in an older style of writing than the body of the text. An occasional first letter is so drowned in squiggles that it can only be interpreted by reference to the rest of the word.

Capital letters are the main stumbling block, since these take many forms, and although writers generally stick to one version per document, so that you can use the Christian name or other known word as clue to the unknown, you may get the awkward cuss who uses more than one form per page, slipping from Secretary to Italic at will. The real brutes are the magistrates or other gentlemen, whose writing is usually for their own eyes. When it is publicly manifest, then people can make the effort to read it or damn them.

Reasonably full alphabets are supplied here, but no one can cover all the forms dreamed up by every individual. If you know what people were taught and the way a lot of people handled this, you should be able to work out what even the crabbiest writing is trying to convey.

Capital letters (and some others)

Capital letters are looked on as a chance to splurge out, with great festoons of inky twirls and twiddles afflicting the innocent letters. the decoration is usually to the left of (or above/before) the letter, so blanking out the first section may help with the worst excesses.

A: frequently lacks a cross bar. It should be a blunted triangle with a waist, but where this has opened out, the tail of the letter may be carried across the centre to form a bar. There is an odd old style version with an open top and closed bottom, which should have a low bar, like a printed **a.** Without it, it looks like a *U*.

B: may have a lot of superstructure or initial flourish, doubling its size, but put your finger over this, and the basic *B* emerges. However, some *B*'s are incompletely closed, looking like *R*'s or *M*'s.

C: is one of the most troublesome, least modern looking letters. There was a perfectly good plain *C*, sometimes with a diagonal dash, or a little curl above. This was too easy, so it was given a curved back tail, then the front was shortened, so you will often meet what looks like *cL* and a dash.

Alternatively, it was closed to make the common plum shape, with a central vertical, with or without a single diagonal. The showier writers do this without taking the pen off, by swirling the down stroke of the pen round and across the middle. The plum steadily lost its diagonal, tipped sideways, and opened up on its way to modern 'joined up' *C*.

D: is also very varied, but the less obvious forms are like an enlarged open *e* or a figure *8*. The latter is a kind of small *d* writ large.

E: is based on Greek , plus a bundle of twiddles in the middle, and maybe diagonal cut marks. There is a slight look of *C* plus spikes.

F: is commonly the double *ff* form already dealt with, though older documents use a single, forward pointed script *F* and late ones the *J* form *F*.

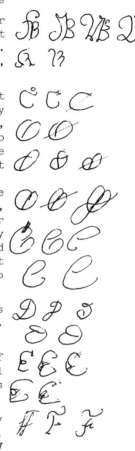

G: can look very much like *C*, only more so - with a double instead of single diagonal, or tilted on its side with a single stroke, but always with a definite extra stroke or curl in its lower section. One style of *G* looks like a Swiss roll in various stages of degeneration and all are more elaborate than the *C* in the same writing.

H: tends to start with a loop above the line, followed by a 'croquet hoop' and a great down curve which may foul the line of writing below. Extra swirls are often met in headings.

The small *h* can be merely the loop and hoop, which looks modern, or the loop and down curve, which looks more like half a paper clip.

J and *I* are regarded as totally interchange-able letters in most cases. If anyone wishes to show a distinction this is generally done by lengthening the down stroke or increasing the top curve of the *J*.

Script forms and looped forms are equally common. The script *J* is often dotted in the middle or crossed. Frequently found is a crossed *I* for *John his mark*.

Small *j* and *i* differ in length, but are interchangeable.

Although *T* should be quite different from *J/I*, having its toe pointing forward, in practice these letters can be very similar, in any style of writing, especially if the cross bar of *J/I* is lost, in italic, or the tail of the *T* is carried across the letter.

K and *R:* with a closed top loop, *K* may look remarkably like an *R* - in fact, more so than most *R*'s - hence the mistaken reading of a girl's name as *Ratheripe* for *Katherine*. The top bar may be thinner than the rest of the loop.

There is a similar form of *R* with a more positive bar (or a smaller loop) and a longer foot curving under the next letters, usually with a stay foot to balance it. More fre-quently, you will meet *R* as a mean little object with a short, goose-stepping foot, jutting down or forward - the latter looks rather like another man's *p* with a dash through, meaning *Par*, though this abbreviation is gen-erally in small letters.

At its most like modern *R*, *K* is partnered by the goose step form of *R* - and the swooping *R* with a *K* with tangled swirls in the middle. Small *k* is a depressed looking letter, as if it has been punched amidships.

M and *W:* bring out the worst among the embellishers, partly because they often start paragraphs. The basic form of *M* is a pair of down curves or spikes, and of *W* an up-spike (*V*) plus an up-curve (*U*). The size of both can be almost doubled by initial twirls and spikes, but whatever happens, the final section of *M* opens upwards and of *W* opens downwards.

N: comes in for something of the same treatment, ending up rather like an **M**. Blank off the first section to read.

P: suffers from initial flourishes, and a prevalent dot in the middle. Sometimes the initial flourish is massive, and the loop tends to break away from the stem, leaving something like a sloppy **Y**. But **Y** always has its short leg to the left of the stem, **P** to the right.

Small **p** has a large initial flourish as normal, or a down stroke and split stem.

R: see with **K**.

S: also has similarities to some types of **c**, being made with a modern style **c** with its tail carried back across the centre. This developed to a modern **S** shape, but, unable to leave well alone, the tail was carried on again to form almost an **8**, or lengthened and twisted round and through.

T: see with **J/I**.
U, V, W: see with **M**.
Y: see with **P**.

Small letters (not already mentioned)

Small letters often surprise us by being joined to the next one at the top instead of the bottom.

One not mentioned above which gives trouble is **c**, reduced from an Elizabethan curve to an angled or vertical short upright, usually thickly written (to distinguish it from **i**). This may be given an initial flourish and joined from the top to the next letter, which makes it look like an **r**. As time goes by, it acquires a lower bar, but may lose the top one or have a flat one appliqued, again looking like an **r**.

Small **r** is generally a double form facing both ways; it degenerates into a **v**. Later it can occur also as a stick with a top curl, and this curl is used in abbreviations with **r**.

Small **t** is often much shorter than we expect, and may not be crossed, or only at the bottom. In older documents, **t** curves over like a **c**.

Long **s** is used for initial and medial letters, as mentioned, and looped **s** for the ends of words. With a projecting tail it looks like **d**, or **e**.

A small **x**, used extensively in numbers, looks a lot like a **p**, but the tail points forward fairly horizontally.

A double **xx** (= 20) above another figure expresses e.g. *iij score* = 60. Notice that the last one of a line of **ii**'s is lengthened. The same applies to the last downstroke of **m** or **n** at the end of a word.

There is a popular 'hatted' style of writing, with round letters given a diagonal or flat tam o'shanter. This is common with **a**, **g**, **d** and accompanied by long initial diagonal tails on **m**, **n**, **u**, **v**, **r**, and also long swooping descenders on **p**, **h**, **s**, **g**, **y** and **z**, which looks pretty as long as the lines are far enough apart for them not to foul each other (see the 1619 will extract, page 17).

Common pairs of letters bring out the worst in regular writers. They are tied together and may lose part of their normal form. You will just have to learn **sh**, **th**, **ch**, **st**, **ct**:

The **th** may look very much like the old English **'thorn'** form, which accounts for the persistence of **ye** for **the**, and the less familiar **yt** and **ys** for **that** and **this**.

Whereas the Churchwardens & Overseers of the poore of the parish of Wendover tid forrens in this County upon due Complaint by them made unto ffrancis Tyrringham & ffrancis Sigo Esq. two of his Majesties Justices of the peace of and for this County (Quorum unus) obteyned an Order or Warrant of Removeall under the hands & seales of the said Justices bearing date the nineteenth day of March last past whereby George Chapman Labourer & Elizabeth his wife & six Children were by them — removed & conveyed from the parish of Wendover tid forrens aforesaid & delivered unto the Officers of the parish of Stoke Mandevile in this County the same then appearing to the said two Justices upon Oath to be the parish place of theire last legall Settlement Now for as much as none of the Officers or Inhabitants of the parish of Stoke Mandevile aforesaid or any other person or persons for them or in theire behalfes have either appeared against or appealed from the said Order or Warrant of Removeall soe made & executed by the said two Justices as aforesaid It is thereupon Ordered by this Court this present Sessions that the said Order or Warrant

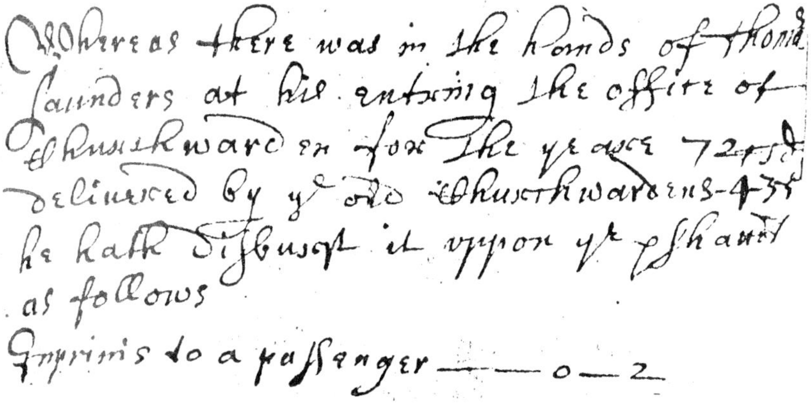

Whereas there was in the hands of Thomas
Saunders at his entring the office of
Churchwarden for the yeare (16)72 £ s d
delivered by the old Churchwardens 4 3 5
he hath disburst it uppon the p(ar)ish and
as follows
Imprimis to a passenger 0 2

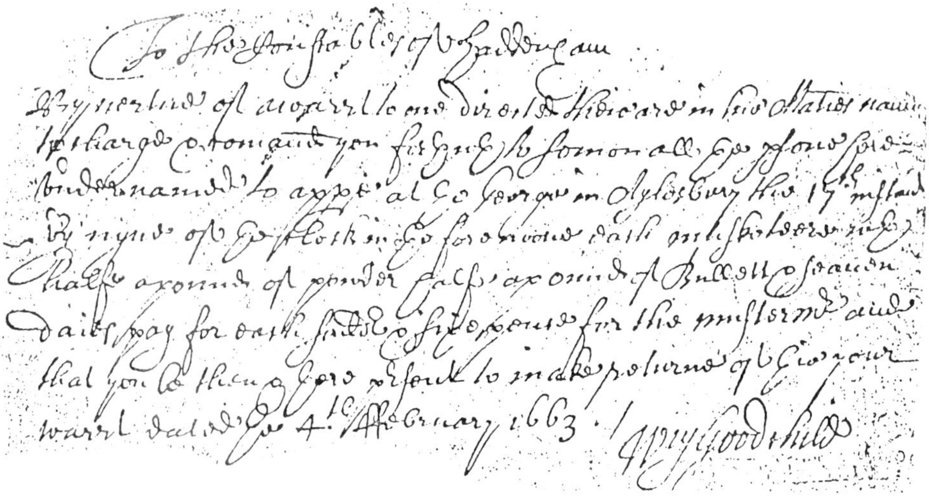

By vertue of a warr(an)t to me directed these are in his Ma(jes)ties name to charge and command you forthw(i)th to somon all the p(er)sons here vnder named to appe(a)r at the George in Aylesbury the 17th instant by nyne of the clocke in the forenoone each musketeere w(i)th halfe a pound of powder halfe a pound of Bullett & seaven daies pay for each sould(ie)r & sixe pense for the musterm(aste)r and that you be then & there p(re)sent to make returne of this your warr(an)t dated the 4th February 1663.

Wm. Goodchilde

Examples of Secretary Hand.

Elizabethan scribes and scribblers

Some of the documents written by people educated before about 1550 may be much more readable to the modern eye than those of a later date, since many official ones were written in a neat 'script' hand which has many basic letters in common with 'modern' script form. This does lead the unwary into confidently starting to search a register from the beginning, only to be utterly bemused by the convoluted writing revealed a few pages later.

Most people should be able to manage the professionally scribed registers of All Saints, Oxford (opposite), for example. Enough decoration is there to make the result attractive, but it is restrained to neat little loops, embellishing a very clear main letter, or bar strokes well out of the way. The writer in 1559 even contrives to distinguish between *J* and *I*. If he had been sloppier, there could have been doubt if *Jacobus Ince* was *James Juce* or *Juer* or *Iver*.

The characteristic differences involve the general look of the page. There is a type of writing with a spiky look to letters like *a, n, u, d, y*, etc., which we expect to be rounded. This may be combined with the 'hat on the side of the head' look mentioned earlier. Instead of curved joining strokes, there are thin pointed lines, which sometimes fade before the rest does. The writer may add to the spiky look with narrow pointed down loops on *h, p, g, q, x, y, z* and long tails on *s, f* and *j*.

'New' letters to watch for are long-tailed *r*'s:

and *r*'s shaped like a *z*:

small *t*'s curved over like a *c*:

and *d*'s with an exaggerated backward loop:

Small *v* is very much like a script *b*:

while *b* is fully looped:

Some letters with loops, or pairs of letters, are perversely tilted into each other: st ld ft

Double *ss* characteristically has one *s* piggybacked on another, and *ff* is similar, plus a cross bar: ss ff

w lives up to its name, sometimes having two *u*'s or *v*'s written over each other:

All Saints', Oxford, registers, 1567.

All Saints', Oxford, registers, 1620.

Will of Richard Webster, 1619.

Will of John Barker, 1559.

An
alphabet
of
around
1600.

A

B

C

D

E

F

G

H

sh ꝯ = the ꝴ ch

I/J

ꝩ ꝩ ÿ = ii

K

L (final)

M

N (nn)

O

P

Q (Scots)=while

R

S final final es double ss
is

T

U/V

W

X

Y z

A real problem may arise with clerks using the old Law Hand, which is imitation medieval. The general effect is of large letters, close together, thick uprights with few or no joining lines, and very odd Gothic capitals. This style was used deliberately for charters and deeds concerning institutions, where impressive appearance was more important than legibility, so that the relevance to the average family history search is not great. The bastard form occasionally used well after 1550 can be an absolute nightmare, if it has decorative twiddles and abbreviations plastered all over it. The 'Gothic' type still used for invitations is almost as bad, but we know what ought to be there, so can cope with it.

Abbreviations

Abbreviations are commonly used – often skied above the general line of letters, which sometimes run them into the line above.

w^{ch} = *which* w^{th} = *with* af^{sd} = *aforesaid*

Ho^{ble} = *Honorable* O^r = *Orator* Matie = *Majesty*

als = *alias* $\overline{Dns}$ = *Dominus, Sir* $\overline{Dna}$ = *Domina, Lady*

$a^o\ \overline{dni}$ = *anno domini, in the year of (our) Lord*

The *p* set, should be:
1. *par* or *per*; 2. *pro*; 3. *pre* or *prae*;
but they are often used indiscriminately. Look out for surnames with contractions in:

Coop = *Cooper* Buckmr = *Buckmaster*

Final *m*, *n* and *r* are often omitted, shown by a curved up tail. Any nasal can be omitted in a word, and should be (but isn't always) replaced by a line over the top:

shearman *considering*

Words regularly used in a particular context, especially a legal one, can be reduced unmercifully.

Adcon is short for **Administration** (later commonly abbreviated to *Admon*).
Words ending in *–ent* or *–ant* lose both letters:

$Testam^t$ = *Testament*; Ten^t = *Tenement* $warr^t$ = *warrant*.

There is also a nasty habit of joining a solitary *a* to the next word, and eliding the *e* in *thelder, thone, thother, thonlie (the only)*.
And is variously expressed at different times by the form known as *ampersand*:

(et) (etc.)

&

At any period, the ends of lines may be filled in with totally meaningless squiggles, to stop cunning persons from adding a word which altered the meaning of a document.

Numbers

Early versions of *1* may have a bent upright, or a lead-in stroke, and tail, which looks like a *2*, and is sometimes dotted:

The *2* is always more definite:

3 can be an emaciated figure, not much more shaped than a *1*, or dropped below the line like a long *z*:

A *5* sometimes loses its top bar, looking like *7*, or has a trailing line making it rather like *6* or *8*.

8 flops sideways, like a depressed *oo*

0 may have a line through it (like a computer *Ø*):

Many numbers, especially for sums of money, are given in Latin:

i, ii, iii, iv or *iiii, v, vi, vii, viii, ix, x, xi, xii*, etc. *xx, xxx, xl (40), l (50), lx (60), lxx, lxxx, xc (90), c (100)*.

The final (or only) *i* was lengthened to *j*:

= *six sheep*   £2. 13s. 4d.

Signs of muddled thinking can be seen in the use of

xxj^{tie} for *21*, obviously thought of as *one and twentie*

and *2°* for *secundo, second*.

Practice makes perfect

The best way to learn to read any handwriting fluently is to do it. Listed opposite are various books of facsimile documents with their transcriptions

Law or Court Hand, used in the seventeenth century
(with acknowledgements to the Borthwick Institute of Historical Research – see Bibliography).